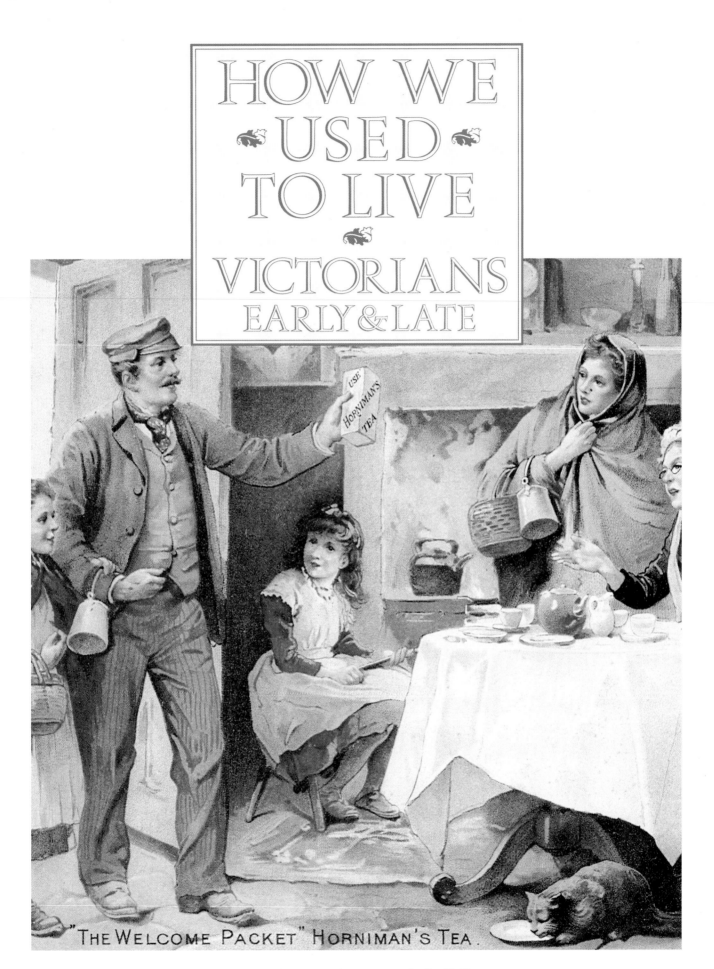

HOW WE USED TO LIVE

VICTORIANS
EARLY & LATE

"THE WELCOME PACKET" HORNIMAN'S TEA.

DAVID EVANS

A & C Black in association with Yorkshire Television

Acknowledgements:

Front Cover: Birmingham Museum and Art Gallery; title page: The Robert Opie Collection p3 Yorkshire Television; p4t Mansell Collection, m David Evans, b Cyfartha Castle Museum/Stephen Done; p5 Mansell Collection; p6t Museum of English Rural Life, b Mansell Collection; p7t National Museum of Wales (Welsh Folk Museum), b Museum of English Rural Life; p8t Yorkshire Television; p9b Birmingham Museum and Art Gallery; p10t Mansell Collection, m Manchester City Art Galleries, b The Post Office, Mary Evans Picture Library; p11t Glasgow Museum of Transport, b Hulton-Deutsch; p12t Mitchell Library, b The Wellcome Institute; p13t The Museum of London, b Beamish; p14t, b Hulton-Deutsch; p15t Mansell Collection, b Hulton-Deutsch; p16t Tim Smith/BHRU, b Quarry Bank Mill Trust Archives (Crown Copyright); p17t Manchester City Art Galleries, b The Robert Opie Collection; p18 Hulton-Deutsch; p19t David Evans, b Barnados; p20t Hulton-Deutsch, b Mansell Collection; p21t Hulton-Deutsch, m The Science Museum, b Mary Evans Picture Library; p22l Hulton-Deutsch, r Mansell Collection; p23t Hulton-Deutsch, b Mansell Collection; p24t Hulton-Deutsch, m The Robert Opie Collection, b The Walker Art Gallery; p25t Mansell Collection, b Hulton-Deutsch; p26t The Wellcome Institute, b Mansell Collection; p27t The Science Museum, b Beamish; p28l Beamish, r York Castle Museum; p29t The Edinburgh Museum of Childhood, b The National Trust Photographic Library; p30t&b Hulton-Deutsch; p31t The Punch Cartoon Library, b Hulton-Deutsch; p32t The Robert Opie Collection, l The Science Museum, r The Robert Opie Collection; p33t Beamish, b The Science Museum, r The Robert Opie Collection; p34t Mary Evans Picture Library, b Manchester City Art Galleries; p35t The Punch Cartoon Library, b Hulton-Deutsch; p36t Hulton-Deutsch, b St John's House, Warwick; p37t Hulton-Deutsch, b The Glamorgan Archive Service; p38t The National Railway Museum, m Hulton-Deutsch, b Mansell Collection; p39t Hulton-Deutsch, b Private Collection; p40l Birmingham Museum and Art Gallery r Woodmansterne; p41t Mansell Collection, b Mary Evans Picture Library; p42t Sheffield City Art Galleries b The Whit Library, Courtauld Institute; p43t Hulton-Deutsch, b Mansell Collection; p46 Mansell Collection, b Hulton-Deutsch; p47t Mary Evans Picture Library, b Hulton-Deutsch; Illustrations on pages 8, 30/31, 40/41 and 46/47 by Mark Peppé.

Designed by Michael Leaman

The front cover shows a detail from 'To Brighton and Back for 3/6' by Charles Rossiter, by courtesy of the Birmingham Museum and Art Gallery.

How We Used to Live is a Yorkshire Television production. Producer/Directors Carol Wilks and Ian Fell.

Contents

A CIP catalogue record for this book is available from the British Library.

ISBN 0-7136-3310-7

First published 1990 by A & C Black (Publishers) Ltd
35 Bedford Row, London WC1R 4JH

Text copyright © 1990 by David Evans

Reprinted 1992 (twice), 1993

Typeset by Method Ltd, Epping, Essex
Printed in Hong Kong for Imago Publishers Ltd

A New Queue

Every day, thousands of visitors to London arrive at Victoria Station or Victoria Coach Station. During their stay, they may visit the Victoria and Albert Museum or the Royal Victoria and Albert Docks. In the evening, they may go to a concert at the Royal Albert Hall. In London alone there are hundreds of reminders of the reign of Queen Victoria and her husband Prince Albert. Are there any streets or buildings in your town that are named after Victoria and Albert?

By the time Victoria died in 1901, Britain was a great industrial country, the centre of a huge empire, and one of the richest and most powerful nations in the world.

The era to which Victoria gave her name began in 1837 when she was 18 years old. On 20th June, she wrote in her diary:

> 'I was awoke at 6 o'clock by Mamma who told me that the Archbishop of Canterbury and Lord Conyngham were here and wished to see me. Lord Conyngham then acquainted me that my poor Uncle, the King, was no more, and had expired at 12 minutes past 2 this morning and consequently that I am Queen.'

In 1840, Victoria married her German cousin Prince Albert. The royal couple's style of family life was eagerly copied by many people. During Victoria's reign, a new social class began to form in Britain – the middle class. These prosperous people wanted to be thought of as 'respectable' members of society. They went to church, gave expensive dinner parties, dressed smartly and brought up their children strictly.

However it was not until late in the Victorian period that these 'Victorian values' began to include a concern for the many people in Britain who were sick, homeless or unemployed. Until then the upper and middle classes preferred to ignore the sufferings of the working class people who worked in appalling conditions and lived in poverty.

▼ This scene from the Yorkshire Television series *How We Used to Live*, takes place in the 1840s. Gideon Harrap has arrived to help his father Daniel to look after the Coggans children who are Daniel's grandchildren. Daniel rescued the children from the workhouse, where they had been sent after their mother died and their father was transported to Australia for being involved in a Chartist riot.

Troubled Times

When Queen Victoria came to the throne, there were about 24 million people living in Great Britain, which at that time included the whole of Ireland as well as Scotland, Wales and England. During the early years of Victoria's reign, new machines were being invented and huge factories built to house them.

▲ In Britain's industrial towns, factories were surrounded by rows of terraced houses.

Steam-powered machines had begun to turn out more goods than ever before. Greater quantities of coal were needed for smelting the iron and steel which were used to make these machines and to provide fuel for steam engines. This period of change which began in the late 1700s, was known as the Industrial Revolution.

Because little work was available in the country areas, many people moved to the towns to find jobs in the new factories. The factory owners built houses for their workers in rows of small, back-to-back terraces. It seemed, said a doctor, that the aim was to 'build the largest number of cottages in the smallest available space'.

▼ Cyfartha Castle in Merthyr Tydfil was the home of the owner of one of the town's iron works. It overlooked the cramped and overcrowded houses of the iron workers.

▲ A Chartist demonstration. The Chartists' list of demands included a vote for every man over 21 and the chance to vote in secret.

The industrial towns were overcrowded and insanitary. In these conditions, diseases like cholera were common and spread quickly through the streets. Waste tips began to build up and factory chimneys belched smoke which polluted the air.

In Victorian Britain, the upper class lived in grand style and the middle class enjoyed comfortable lives, but things were very different for the working class. Men, women and children had to work long hours for low wages and many families could barely afford basic food and clothing. Bread was expensive because of the Corn Laws, which had placed a tax on grain imported from abroad.

In an age when there was no social security, people lived in dread of losing their job, falling sick and growing old. Benjamin Disraeli, who became prime minister in 1868, described Britain as:

'Two nations, between whom there is no contact and no sympathy; we are as ignorant of each other's habits, thoughts and feelings, as if we were dwellers in different zones, or inhabitants of different planets.'

Working people did not have the right to vote and had no say in the running of the country. In the early part of Victoria's reign, a group of men tried to change this. Led by William Lovett and Feargus O'Connor, they made a list of complaints against Parliament and called it a 'People's Charter'. The Chartists, as they became known, presented a petition to Parliament, claiming it was supported by five million signatures. In fact, it had less than half that number and included many obvious forgeries. It was signed by 'Mr Punch', 'Queen Victoria' and by 'the Duke of Wellington' no less than 18 times! The Chartists were made to look ridiculous and their movement ended in failure.

When Victoria became queen, Britain already controlled a huge empire which included Canada, India, Australia and New Zealand. These countries provided Britain with raw materials like cotton and wool which British factories made into manufactured goods like clothes. These goods were then sold throughout the empire, making more money for Britain. The Victorians were very proud of their empire. It was so vast that they claimed it was an empire 'on which the sun never set.'

Country Life

As the number of people in Britain began to increase, more food was needed to feed them. Farmers were able to produce this extra food by using new machinery and improved ways of growing crops and rearing animals. These farmers became very wealthy, but the labourers who worked for them stayed poor.

▲ A Victorian cartoon comparing the prosperity of a farmer with the poverty of his labourer.

Farm work was hard and the labourers had to work outside in all sorts of weather. Apart from labouring, there were jobs which needed special skills such as hedging, ditching and shearing. Men also worked as ploughmen, shepherds and cowmen. Wages were low and varied from 7 shillings (35p) to 12 shillings (60p) a week. This was at a time when butter cost 1 shilling (5p) a pound and tea cost 1 shilling for a quarter pound, and farm workers often had large families to feed. Extra money could be earned at haytime, harvesting and shearing, but farm workers' pay was still less than the earnings of factory workers.

Women were employed as farm workers and did the same work as the men. They also helped with the milking, made butter and cheese in the dairy and did other domestic work. Even young children were found odd-jobs. In the spring, they were sometimes used as scarecrows!

▼ A farm worker's family crowd together in their sparsely furnished cottage.

Farm labourers and their families had few comforts. Farm cottages were made of stone and had thatched roofs. They had one bedroom with a living room below and were damp, cramped and overcrowded. The labourer's cottage was 'tied', which meant that it belonged to his employer. The tenant would pay a low rent or no rent at all, but if he moved or lost his job, he would have to leave his home.

Some farm workers wore smocks, but most wore a shirt, waistcoat and breeches, trousers which were cut off just below the knee. Leggings were worn to cover the legs below the knees. Workers ate their mid-day meal of bread, cheese and ale in the field. At home, they enjoyed the perk of having fresh farm produce to eat.

Country life had its lighter moments, too. Villagers took part in religious festivals and seasonal events. After a successful harvest, everyone celebrated with a harvest supper. At Christmas time, carollers visited the village and people ate a special meal of roast beef and plum pudding. At other times, there was morris dancing, maypole dancing and 'guising', when the children of the village paraded through the streets wearing animal masks.

There were often arguments between farmers and their low-paid workers. In 1834, six labourers from Tolpuddle in Dorset were transported to Australia for trying to form a trade union. The number of farm labourers dropped steadily during the second half of the 1800s. The population of rural Britain fell as people left the country areas to look for work in the factory towns.

▼ A Staffordshire village's annual horn dance.

Transport and Communication

The first stretch of railway line in Britain was opened in 1825. It joined Stockton with Darlington and was 14 kilometres long. There followed a period of frantic railway building which reached its height during the 1840s, the period of 'railway mania'. By 1900, Britain was covered by a railway network with over 29,000 kilometres of track.

The famous railway engineers were Richard Trevithick, William Hedley, Isambard Kingdom Brunel and George Stephenson and his son, Robert. The railways were built by gangs of men called railway navvies. Experienced in blasting and tunnelling, they were paid twice the wages of other labourers. They dressed in moleskin trousers and multi-coloured waistcoats with gaudy handkerchiefs around their necks and were known by their nicknames – 'Fighting Jack', 'Gipsy Joe' and 'Thicklipped Blondin'. A popular navvies' song went:

'I've navvied here in Scotland, I've navvied in the south,
Without a drop to cheer me or a crust to cross me mouth,
I fed when I was workin' and starved when out on tramp,
And the stone has been me pillow and the moon above me lamp.'

Many people were opposed to the railways. Some claimed that the tracks and embankments would scar the countryside. Others argued that the environment would suffer because of the noise, smoke and dirt. Farmers complained because they feared the steam engines would frighten their animals.

▲ The British railway network in 1847.

The first train averaged 19 kilometres an hour and had to stop at every station. Passengers travelled in First, Second or Third Class carriages. First Class passengers enjoyed the comfort of well-padded seats and a roof as protection against the weather; Third Class passengers had no seats and had to hold on tightly to a handrail. A railway travellers' handbook advised men to guard their wallets in tunnels and suggested that women put pins in their mouths to avoid being kissed by male passengers! By 1870, elegant Pullman carriages were in use with buffet cars and sleepers.

The coming of the railways changed the daily lives of everyone in Britain. Passengers and goods could be transported more quickly across the country, and fresh foods such as fish and vegetables could be sent to distant markets and arrive in good condition. New 'railway towns' like Darlington, Crewe and Swindon where the locomotives were built grew in size and importance. Rural areas were easier to get to. People would 'save up' to take their annual holidays in popular resorts such as Brighton, Blackpool and Margate. Cuttings, tunnels, embankments and bridges became familiar features of the British landscape.

▲ A poster advertising a rail excursion to the Great Exhibition at Crystal Palace.

▼ Cheap railway fares made it possible for people to travel more widely and enjoy day trips.

9

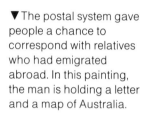

▼The postal system gave people a chance to correspond with relatives who had emigrated abroad. In this painting, the man is holding a letter and a map of Australia.

In the towns, horses were the main form of transport. Horse-drawn hansom cabs and hackney coaches were common on city streets. Horse-drawn buses carried passengers both inside and on the roof. In 1891 the first electric trams appeared on the streets of London. They were faster and cleaner than horse-drawn buses and could carry more passengers. By the time Queen Victoria died in 1901, electric trams had almost completely replaced horse-drawn buses. In 1863, the first underground railway was opened in London.

A Penny Black ▶

POSTAGE
ONE PENNY

The new railways meant that letters and parcels could be sent quickly round the country. The 'Penny Post' was started in 1840 by Rowland Hill. The first postage stamp was known as the Penny Black. Regular postal deliveries meant that householders had to put letter boxes in their front doors. After 1876, Victorians were also able to communicate with each other by telephone.

Trains also brought newspapers and magazines to villages and towns all over the country. Newspapers had existed since the early 1700s, in a weekly or monthly form, but it was not until 1855 that the first daily morning paper 'The Daily Telegraph' was published. It used large, banner headlines which some people thought were 'lacking in moderation and respect.' A popular one penny magazine was 'Tit-Bits'. In 1896, Alfred Harmsworth launched the 'Daily Mail'. He called it 'a penny newspaper selling for a halfpenny' and it was a great success.

▲Post boxes were first introduced in London in 1855.

Other new inventions included the safety bicycle, which replaced the wooden-wheeled 'boneshaker' and the 'penny-farthing', and towards the end of the century, the motor car. At first, these inventions were made by hand and so only very rich people could afford to buy them. The first motor cars or 'horseless carriages' were limited to a maximum speed of 6 kilometres an hour and had to be preceded by a man carrying a red flag.

▲ A Scottish motor car, built in 1895. Although its top speed was 17 miles per hour, its owner was fined for speeding.

▼ At first, only very wealthy people could afford to own a telephone. The early telephone exchanges were operated by hand. They provided jobs for many women.

Townspeople and City Life

The families who had poured into the towns to look for work in the factories were housed in hastily and cheaply built rows of back-to-back terraced houses. These houses were built close to the factories in the centre of the towns.

Ventilation and lighting were poor and, as there was no protection against damp, water trickled down the walls. The front doors opened onto the street and the houses had small backyards which led to narrow alleyways.

There were no inside toilets; instead, people had to use outdoor 'earth closets' above cesspits, which were shared by several households. The foul-smelling cesspits were emptied after dark by 'night men'. Water came from street taps or was carried in buckets from a nearby river.

Sewage often seeped into the water supplies, which led to the rapid spread of diseases. The maze of streets and alleys were filthy, rat-infested and disease ridden. Many people died from consumption or tuberculosis, and there were outbreaks of infectious diseases like cholera and typhoid.

▲ There was little daylight or fresh air in the alleyway between these tall, closely-built houses in Glasgow.

▼ Women and children collect water from a standpipe in the street.

Some factory owners thought that their employees would work harder and produce more goods if they were provided with healthier and more comfortable working conditions. Robert Owen, a factory owner at New Lanark in Scotland, believed that squalid working and living conditions robbed people of their self respect and sometimes even turned them into criminals. Owen treated his workers well, built them decent homes and even provided a school for their children.

William and James Lever, the soapmakers, built a village for their workers which they called Port Sunlight. They provided their employees with good housing, medical care and a share of the company's profits.

By day, the streets of Britain's cities and towns bustled with activity. In a typical row of shops there would be a tailor, a draper selling fabric, a shoemaker, a barber and of course, a grocer. The grocer's shop might be one of a chain of shops started by Thomas Lipton, or it might be a co-operative.

▲ In a grocery shop, each customer was served individually by a shop assistant.

▲ The draper's department of a co-operative store. Co-ops were particularly popular with working class people.

Co-operatives were popular because the people who ran them shared their profits with their customers. Groceries were sold 'loose' and each item had to be weighed and wrapped. Liquids were measured into jugs and bottles provided by the customer.

In the streets, stall-holders, pedlars and costermongers selling fruit and vegetables competed with each other as they shouted out their wares – 'Lovely sweet violets', 'Muffins for sale', 'Oysters', 'Hot eels' and 'Milko – a penny a pint'. Knives were sharpened in the street and shoe-blacks and menders of all kinds touted for business. Beggars and pickpockets mingled among the buskers, street musicians, organ grinders and hurdy-gurdy men.

The streets themselves were filthy, as there were no proper sewers or drains, and the air was polluted by the smoke from the factory chimneys. The coming of the omnibuses and trams meant that people who could afford to commute to work could move away from the overcrowded and dirty town centres. These people moved to the edge of the towns where the air was cleaner. Factory owners and rich businessmen owned fine homes well away from the towns.

◄On the quayside of this busy British port goods are loaded and unloaded from a queue of waiting ships.

British engineers used what they had learned from building train engines to build engines for ships. By 1900, 75% of all the world's steamships were built in Britain. Goods were sent abroad and raw materials brought to the country in these steamships.

As workers and their families moved to the new industrial centres, villages grew into towns and towns developed into sprawling cities. Bradford, Leeds and Manchester became important textile towns, Sheffield won a world-wide reputation for its stainless steel cutlery and Stoke-on-Trent, centre of 'The Potteries', became famous for its pottery and porcelain.

In 1851, the Great Exhibition was held in London. It was the idea of Prince Albert and was intended to display the 'Works of Industry of all Nations'. It was really a chance for British manufacturers to show off their goods and the quality of their craftsmanship.

The exhibition was held in Hyde Park in a magnificent building made entirely of glass and iron which was called the Crystal Palace. The public had the chance to see over 100,000 exhibits, which included textiles, furniture, machinery and household goods. People from all over the country came to visit the unusual building and see the exhibits.

The Workshop of the World

Britain's growing population not only needed more food, it also needed more clothing, household tools such as cutlery, china and pottery and manufactured goods such as furniture and beds. Large numbers of men, women and children workers were employed in the factories to produce these goods, which the railways moved around the country to markets and ports.

▼Huge crowds celebrate the launch of the Great Britain. In 1845 it reached New York from Liverpool in 14½ days.

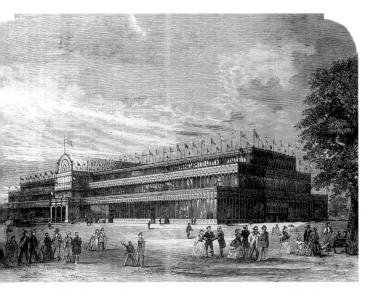

▲ The Crystal Palace took only six months to build. A newspaper at the time called it a 'Marvel of Modern Engineering'.

▼ The hardware section of the Great Exhibition where goods made of metals such as copper and iron were displayed.

Railway companies offered people the chance to buy special excursion tickets and travel cheaply to London. Some people turned the visit into a social occasion. Clergymen organised parties and factory owners even gave their workers a day off and paid for both the trip and their admission. In the six months that it was open, the Great Exhibition was visited by over six million people.

By the 1850s, Britain had become the world's greatest trading nation, with the value of goods produced by British industries increasing by over £10 million each year. Middle class people began to set up small businesses or to enter skilled professions like teaching and medicine. People who could afford it moved away from the centres of the towns and bought houses in the more pleasant suburbs away from the grime of the factories.

Although Britain's increased prosperity as a nation helped to create a huge new middle class of people, it did nothing to narrow the divide between the lives of very rich and very poor people. It was still wealth for the few and poverty for the many.

A Day in the Life of a Factory Worker

For most of the year, a worker would have to rise well before dawn. Like other men on his shift, he would be woken up by the 'knocker-up', who would tap on his bedroom window. The 'knocker-up' was often the factory overseer. It was part of his job to make sure that each shift arrived for work on time. Workers who arrived late at the factory were fined, or could even lose their job.

Many families took in lodgers and the house would be particularly crowded at breakfast time. At best, there would be porridge, bread and tea for breakfast. The wife of a worker might also work at the factory. Women often took in work at home, such as washing and sewing. Many children of nine or over would go to the factory with their father. Any children who stayed at home would be looked after by the eldest child or would spend the day in the streets.

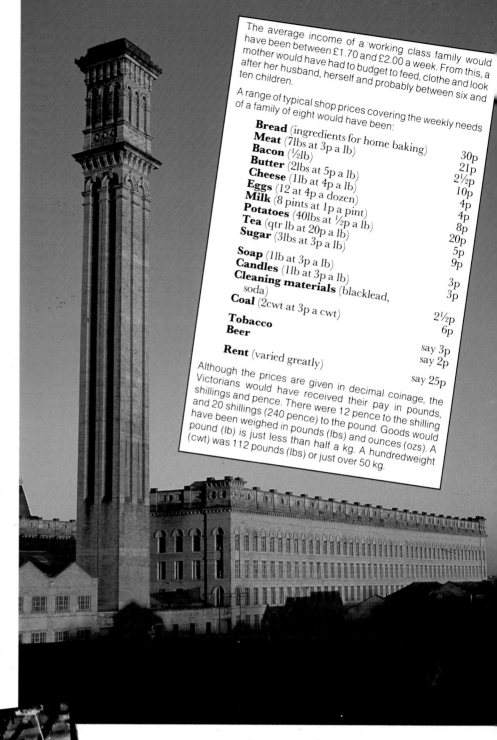

The average income of a working class family would have been between £1.70 and £2.00 a week. From this, a mother would have had to budget to feed, clothe and look after her husband, herself and probably between six and ten children.

A range of typical shop prices covering the weekly needs of a family of eight would have been:

Bread (ingredients for home baking)	30p
Meat (7lbs at 3p a lb)	21p
Bacon (½lb)	2½p
Butter (2lbs at 5p a lb)	10p
Cheese (1lb at 4p a lb)	4p
Eggs (12 at 4p a dozen)	4p
Milk (8 pints at 1p a pint)	8p
Potatoes (40lbs at ½p a lb)	20p
Tea (qtr lb at 20p a lb)	5p
Sugar (3lbs at 3p a lb)	9p
Soap (1lb at 3p a lb)	3p
Candles (1lb at 3p a lb)	3p
Cleaning materials (blacklead, soda)	
Coal (2cwt at 3p a cwt)	2½p
Tobacco	6p
Beer	
Rent (varied greatly)	say 3p
	say 2p
	say 25p

Although the prices are given in decimal coinage, the Victorians would have received their pay in pounds, shillings and pence. There were 12 pence to the shilling and 20 shillings (240 pence) to the pound. Goods would have been weighed in pounds (lbs) and ounces (ozs). A pound (lb) is just less than half a kg. A hundredweight (cwt) was 112 pounds (lbs) or just over 50 kg.

▲ A textile mill in Bradford. Poor ventilation and lighting together with overcrowding and the deafening noise of machinery made factory conditions hardly bearable.

◄ Machinery was left unguarded so there was always the risk of serious injury.

Factory work was hard and boring. The safer working conditions provided by some factory owners like Robert Owen were the exception to the rule. While men and women worked at the machines, children were given jobs like cleaning and carrying. If they stopped for a rest, they were beaten.

The most cruelly treated factory workers were the pauper apprentices. These were the homeless and orphaned children who worked for the factory owners.

Factories were run by strict rules and workers were watched by stern overseers. Workers could be fined for laziness, talking, damaging machinery or even for not being washed. In textile mills and coal mines, smoking was punished with instant dismissal. Although laws had been passed to limit the number of hours worked by women and children, they did not apply to men. It was not unusual for a man to work twelve hours a day and sometimes even longer. Workers returned to their homes totally exhausted.

Wages varied in different industries. Until 1824, workers were punished as criminals if they tried to form trade unions. Even after that, unions were weak and few men dared to strike. It was not until later in the century that unions were able to begin to work to improve the conditions of low-paid and unskilled workers. Even when unions were legalised, they had to fight to make employers listen to them. In 1842, a mill worker earned 10 shillings (50p) a week and his wife considerably less.

▲ At noon, factory workers were given an hour for dinner. They ate bread and cheese and drank cold tea.

Children were paid according to their age – 3 shillings and threepence (17p) for a nine-year-old, rising to 7 shillings (35p) at the age of fifteen. Some factory owners operated the 'truck system' by which workers received part of their pay in tokens. These could only be spent at the shop owned by the factory owner.

Away from the factory, workers often relaxed in the pub. Others spent the evening studying or teaching themselves to read.

▼ This advertisement for tea paints a very unrealistic picture of a worker's return home. At the end of a shift, workers were dirty and exhausted.

Paupers and Workhouses

As long ago as 1601, a law was passed which made each parish responsible for its own poor. To cope with the problem, parishes paid charity or 'outdoor relief' to those who were able to live at home. They provided 'indoor relief' for those with nowhere to go by admitting them into parish workhouses. These workhouses were built with money from the rates, which were paid by people who owned land or a house. They were overcrowded, squalid places which provided very inadequate shelter for their inmates.

In 1834, the system of indoor and outdoor relief changed There was a common belief in Victorian times that paupers (people who needed help from the parish) were lazy scroungers. Now all the poor were made to live in the workhouse. The parish workhouses were replaced by bigger ones taking the poor from a larger area. Boards of guardians were elected to supervise the workhouses, which had to be regularly inspected.

▲ Dinnertime in the women's section of a workhouse. Often, inmates were fed on gruel, a thin porridge made by boiling oatmeal in milk or water.

To discourage people from entering the workhouse, conditions were deliberately made extremely harsh. A clergyman who thought that poverty was the same as idleness, said:

'The workhouse should be a place of hardship, of coarse fare, of shame and humility; it should be administered with strictness – with severity; it should be as repulsive as is consistent with humanity'.

Husbands and wives were separated, no visitors were allowed and the able-bodied were given very grim work to do. They had to break stones, chop wood or crush bones to make glue. The food was plain and had to be eaten in silence. In one place, inmates were fed in a trough, like pigs. Accommodation was sparse, cold and uncomfortable.

Apart from the poor, the workhouses took in sick, old and insane people. They were all kept together; only the men and women were separated. Inmates were often bullied and beaten. Those who misbehaved or were found drunk were punished with solitary confinement and a reduction in their food.

At Andover in Hampshire, the workhouse was run by a cruel drunkard. Starving inmates ate the rotten meat that was left on the bones which had been sent to the workhouse to be crushed. These dreadful places were known as 'Bastilles' after the notorious prison in Paris which had a reputation for appalling conditions. The conditions inside the workhouses were so awful that some people preferred to starve to death rather than enter them.

When the scandalous conditions at Andover were made known, the government took action and made sure that workhouses were run according to regulations. Some people decided to use their time and money to help the poor. In London, a home for destitute children was opened by Doctor Barnado, and William Booth founded the Salvation Army to work among the poor and 'take the gospel of love to the slums'.

▲ The infamous Andover workhouse as it is today. The building is now part of a college. Are there any old workhouses in your town? What are they used for today?

▼ In the homes set up by Dr Barnado, orphaned children were taught skills like carpentry, which would help them find jobs when they were older.

Crime and Criminals

During Victorian times, poverty and grim living conditions often drove people to commit crimes. House breaking, theft and assault were common. In towns and cities, pickpockets, swindlers and forgers mingled with the crowds on the streets. Without a proper police force, criminals were seldom caught.

Those who were caught were severely punished. The upper classes were determined to protect their possessions and keep working class people 'in their place'. Laws were passed which punished crimes against property more severely than crimes against other people. Depending on their crime, men and women could be flogged, imprisoned, sent as convicts to Australia or sentenced to death by hanging. Until 1844, people owing even small amounts of money were sent to a debtors' prison. The transportation of convicts to Australia ended in the 1840s, but public hangings continued well into the 1860s. These brutal executions attracted huge crowds, with much singing, drinking and fighting.

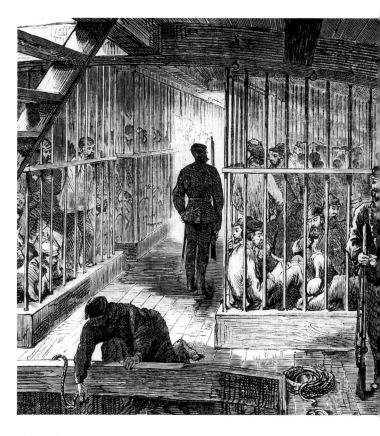

▲Conditions were so harsh inside convict ships bound for Australia, that many prisoners died during the voyage.

In early Victorian gaols, prisoners were crammed together in foul-smelling rooms and were often beaten and starved by their gaolers. It is said that at one prison the convicts were so badly fed that they ate live worms and frogs; in another, they melted candles into their soup to make it more nourishing. As gaolers were unpaid, they made money by threatening, bullying and blackmailing the prisoners.

Later in Victoria's reign, changes were made which aimed to reform as well as punish prisoners. After 1840, when the Australians in New South Wales refused to accept any more convicts, new prisons had to be built in Britain. In these prisons, convicts were given a clean cell each, but were made to live in complete isolation from each other. Some prisoners who could not face the loneliness went mad or even tried to kill themselves.

Under the 'silent system', convicts had to remain absolutely quiet at all times – even when they were working, eating or at exercise. Sometimes prisoners at exercise would be made to wear masks so that they could not recognise or talk to one another. Those who broke the silence were placed in solitary confinement and given a bread and water diet.

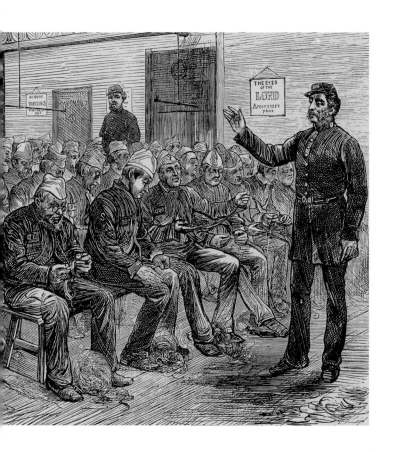

▲Convicts were made to untwist old rope for hours on end. This boring work made their fingers red and raw.

Pub. by R.Ackermann, London.   TREAD MILL.

Towards the end of the century, conditions did begin to improve. A report published in 1898 said that the aim of prisons should be to reform prisoners and 'turn them out better men and women than when they came in'.

As a result of the report, prisons began to be regularly inspected. Women prisoners were separated from the men and looked after by female warders. All convicts were seen by a doctor and visited by a prison chaplain. The report said that prisoners should be given more rewarding work to do and taught to read and write, although this was only put into practice in a few prisons. The gaolers, or turnkeys as they had been called, were replaced by paid warders. Prisoners were rewarded for good behaviour by having their sentences reduced.

▲ Prisoners had to walk a treadmill or 'everlasting staircase' like this one as part of their daily routine.

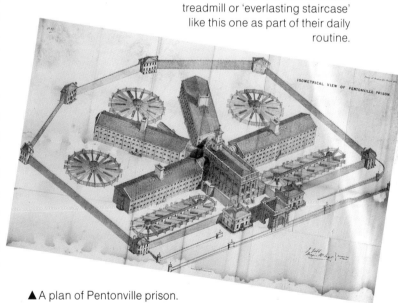

▲ A plan of Pentonville prison.

◄ The first policemen were known as Bow Street Runners. After 1829, they wore uniforms and were nicknamed Peelers or Bobbies after their founder, Robert Peel.

21

◀A family look through their photograph collection. The camera first came into use in the 1840s. Victorians enjoyed having their picture taken.

Servants were cheap and every family had at least one maid. In some households, there would be a butler, parlour and housemaids, a cook and possibly a gardener. Once the cleaning was done, the servants would stay 'downstairs' in the basement until a bell summoned them 'upstairs'.

Upstairs, Downstairs

For the upper and middle classes, Queen Victoria's reign was a period of comfortable living and prosperity. The ladies and gentlemen of the upper class were the leaders of society. Surrounded by servants, they lived pampered lives on their country estates.

The middle class covered a wide range of people, from lawyers, doctors and bankers to shopkeepers, teachers and clerks. By our standards, these middle class Victorians may seem strict, narrow minded and over interested in being considered 'respectable'. They tried to copy the lifestyles of the upper classes and do nothing that would cause their friends and neighbours to gossip about them.

Father, called 'papa' by his children, earned the money which was needed to support his family and was head of the household. He sat at the head of the table, carved the meat on Sunday and led the family in their daily prayers. Mother, 'mama', was expected to be domesticated and meek. She was responsible for raising the children and day-to-day management of the home. Children had to be obedient and respectful. A popular Victorian saying was that 'children should be seen and not heard'. They were often cared for by a nanny.

▲ Servants were often very badly paid, but they were given food, clothing and a room to live in.

▶ Children being presented to their parents' guests before a dinner party. Nanny carries the youngest child.

While fathers and sons worked to achieve success, mothers and daughters were expected to become 'accomplished' – able to sing, play the piano or produce fine embroidery. Marriage was meant to be the aim of every girl. Courtship began when a young man asked for 'permission to call'. The young couple would always be accompanied or 'chaperoned'. Eventually, he would ask for the girl's 'hand in marriage'. Before agreeing, her father would ask the young man about his job, salary and future prospects.

The household followed a daily routine. Meals were at fixed times and the family were called to the table by the sounding of a gong. Children were told off if they were late for meals. They were expected to eat up all their food. If they didn't, it would reappear at the next meal.

On winter evenings, the children would play parlour games like dominoes, draughts and ludo. In the summer, they might play croquet on the lawn or go for a bicycle ride.

Victorians enjoyed entertaining at home and gave lavish parties. During the summer months, most families took a holiday. Many went to the seaside and a few very wealthy families even travelled abroad to France or Switzerland.

▲ A family photo of a girl with her mother and grandmother.

Victorian Fashion

The smoke and dirt of factory life made it difficult for working class people to keep their clothes clean. Every piece of clothing had to last as long as possible, becoming shabbier and more patched the longer it was worn. The children of factory workers wore hand-me-downs and many had to go barefoot. Nevertheless, these families followed the Victorian fashion of wanting to 'keep up appearances' and set aside clothes for 'Sunday best'.

For middle class people, the quality and cut of their clothes indicated their place in society. Dressing took a long time. It was fashionable for women to have 'an hour-glass figure'. They made their waists slim by wearing boned corsets. Sometimes the corsets were pulled so tight that they were painful to wear.

▲ A painting called 'Dollmakers and Dollbreakers' contrasts the dress and behaviour of poor and rich children.

Wide skirts called crinolines were very popular. A woman would first put on a hooped frame made of bamboo or whalebone. Over this went several layers of petticoats, the outer ones stiffened with starch. On top of these, she wore a dress made of velvet, silk or taffeta, which was high around the neck, wide at the shoulders and narrow at the waist. From the waist it hung like a bell until it reached the floor. During the 1870s, the crinoline was replaced by a new fashion, the bustle. Layers of material were bunched up at the back of a dress to form a bustle.

▲ A corset advertisement.

► The wealthy family in this painting are being visited by their poor relations. Compare the respectable but plain dress of the one women with the elaborate, expensive dress of the other.

Rich women could afford better quality material and more elaborate dresses, with embroidered pleats, frills and bows. Widows and old women dressed all in black. Outside, women wore felt hats or bonnets and gloves or fur muffs and carried parasols.

During the day, men dressed in coloured waistcoats and dark, knee-length frock coats with elegant trimmings. They wore striped trousers which were fastened by a strap under their shoes. It was fashionable to wear stiff collars with cravats around the neck. Beards and moustaches were very popular.

Underneath their clothes men wore long sleeved vests and long underpants. These were made of wool and, although warm, they were itchy and uncomfortable. Outdoors, men wore bowler or top hats and carried a cane or a walking stick. A Victorian fashion for the Inverness cape and deer-stalker hat was later made famous in the Sherlock Holmes detective stories.

▲ Victorians dressed 'respectably', even on the beach. Bathing costumes covered the body almost from head to toe.

▼ It was difficult for a woman wearing a crinoline to get through a narrow opening like a turnstile.

Sickness and Disease

At the start of Victoria's reign, doctors knew little about the causes of diseases and could only offer simple, painful and often useless remedies. Cautery, or using hot irons to clean wounds and ulcers, and the use of leeches to suck blood were common practices.

Surgery was gruesome. Amputations were done by surgeons dressed in ordinary clothes splattered with the blood of previous patients. Their instruments were not sterilised. Even when patients survived these operations, many still died soon afterwards from gangrene (blood poisoning) or shock. One doctor said:

> 'The man who is stretched on the operating table in one of our hospitals is in far greater danger of dying than was the English soldier on the battlefield of Waterloo.'

Nitrous oxide was used during operations. It made people giggle and was named 'laughing gas'. The anaesthetic effects often wore off before the end of an operation. Surgeons tried ether instead, but found that it made patients sick. So James Simpson's use of chloroform proved to be a major breakthrough. Patients remained unconscious longer and there were no harmful after effects.

Scientists discovered that invisible microbes (germs) infected wounds and caused them to turn septic. The surgeon Joseph Lister used this knowledge to invent a spray which sent a fine mist of carbolic acid, a strong disinfectant, into the air whilst he was operating.

▲ During the Crimean War, Florence Nightingale became responsible for the care of wounded British soldiers. She worked to improve conditions in the military hospital wards, like this one at Scutari in Turkey.

At the start of the 1800s, the first blood transfusions had been attempted, but they were not really safe until after 1900, when it became possible to identify different blood groups. In 1895, the German scientist Wilhelm Röntgen discovered x-rays, which became important in locating diseases and treating broken bones. Three years later, Marie and Pierre Curie discovered radium, which was used in the treatment of cancer. Victorian doctors were helped in their daily work by the invention of the stethoscope and the thermometer.

▼ Lister's carbolic spray in use during an operation. His use of antiseptics made operations much safer.

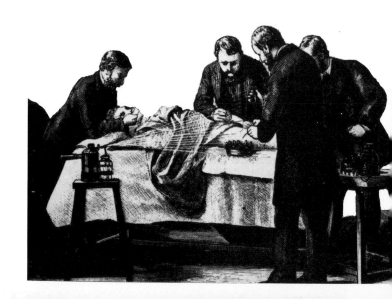

People still continued to fear outbreaks of highly infectious and deadly diseases like cholera, typhus and typhoid. Prince Albert himself died of typhoid fever. By the end of the 1800s, immunisation (making people more resistant to a disease by injecting them with a mild form of that disease) could be used to protect people against cholera and typhoid. However, tuberculosis (a disease affecting the lungs) remained a threat and children's lives were especially at risk from measles and whooping cough.

By the end of Victoria's reign, people were living longer. There were many reasons for this. Housing and sanitation had improved, working hours were reduced, cheap cotton clothes were available, soap was more plentiful and people enjoyed a better diet.

▲Medical students watch an operation at a London hospital in 1895.

▼A dentist's surgery of the late 1800s. Notice the canisters of gas used as an anaesthetic and the foot-operated drill.

Middle Class Homes

The houses of middle class Victorians were much larger and more spacious than the back to back houses of factory workers. You can still see these middle class homes in many towns and cities. Today, they are often divided into offices or flats. These three-storied buildings often had large cellars. Each house had a hedged lawn to the front and a big garden at the back.

On the ground floor, there would be a dining room and a drawing room or parlour and, at the rear, a kitchen, larder and scullery where the washing up was done. The biggest houses also had breakfast rooms and studies. The bedrooms and nursery were on the first floor whilst the servants lived at the top of the house in small attic rooms.

The dining room had a large central table surrounded by upright chairs. The 'carver', a bigger chair with arms, was for the father of the family, who carved the roast at meal times. The drawing room, or parlour, where visitors were entertained, contained leather arm chairs, a settee, sideboards, and a loud ticking grandfather clock. The coming of the railways and the introduction of train timetables had made the Victorians more aware of time.

▲ The centrepiece of a Victorian kitchen was the range. Around a central fire there were baking and roasting ovens and a hot closet to warm plates. The kitchen dresser was loaded with plates and cooking utensils like copper saucepans and frying pans.

Victorian furniture was intended to be elegant but comfortable and was mainly made from dark, heavy woods like mahogany and oak. Above the fireplace was an ornamental mantelpiece cluttered with ornaments, candlesticks and plates. Near the fireplace was a coal scuttle and a poker, shovel and tongs for picking up hot coals. When the fire was unlit, an ornamental fire-screen was placed across the front of the fireplace.

Favourite Victorian ornaments were rounded glass cases containing imitation plants, wax fruit and even stuffed animals. The pictures on the walls were hung in large, heavy frames. Satin and lace curtains hung at the windows. Many Victorians liked to have a large plant called an aspidistra in a pot on the window sill.

◄A reconstruction of a Victorian drawing room at the Castle Museum in York.

▼Rocking horses and indoor see-saws were very popular with Victorian children.

▼A bath and washstand.

Upstairs, the bedrooms would have open fireplaces. The beds, with metal frames and springs, had brass knobs at each corner. At night, the bed would be warmed with a stone bottle filled with hot water. In the bedroom there would also be wardrobes and possibly an ottoman, a cushioned chest which could hold linen and could also be used to sit on.

As few houses had bathrooms, people washed in the bedroom. There was a washstand in each bedroom with a large jug and basin. At bathtime, servants carried a small bath to the bedroom and filled it with hot water, which had to be brought to the room from the kitchen. Improved sanitation meant that most middle class houses had an indoor toilet. Chamber-pots were kept underneath the beds for use during the night.

Working People and the New Laws

After the 1850s, Parliament began to show a greater concern for the welfare of working people. Laws were passed which affected the family both at home and at work.

In 1875, Parliament made every council responsible for drainage, sewage, street cleaning and the supply of fresh water. Health inspectors and sanitary officers were appointed to make sure that the new law was carried out properly. Another law gave councils the right to buy up houses which were 'unfit for human habitation' and knock them down. By the end of the century, councils were able to use money taken from the rates to build new houses – council houses.

DIPHTHERIA   SCROFULA   CHOLERA

▲ The filthy state of the Thames and other rivers made it necessary for Parliament to pass laws to improve ways of disposing of sewage and supplying fresh water.

▲ Many horrific accidents were caused in factories because machinery was left unguarded. Conditions improved when Parliament passed laws which made factory owners responsible for the safety of their workers.

A working class family in the 1880s

Some dishonest bakers, brewers and shopkeepers cheated their customers by putting cheap and sometimes dangerous substances in their food. They added water to milk, plaster of Paris to flour and a chemical called alum to bread to make it whiter. Parliament appointed officers to check goods sold in shops and prosecute offenders.

Laws were passed which limited the number of hours women and children could work. The employment of women and boys under ten in coal mines was banned altogether. Even so, after 1874 children aged over nine could still be employed in factories and women were expected to work a ten hour day.

▲ This cartoon from 1867 shows that many in Parliament were opposed to giving the vote to working class men. They saw it as 'a leap in the dark'. Nevertheless, in 1884, all men were given the right to vote.

I belong to a trade union at work. And I can vote in elections.

I can stay on at school until I'm ten.

After the 1860s, trade unions were allowed to exist, but these 'New Model Unions' were mainly for skilled workers. In 1875, workers won the right to bargain with their employers and even to strike as long as their picketing was peaceful. Shortly afterwards, London dockers successfully went on strike for a wage of sixpence an hour.

At the beginning of Victoria's reign, working class men did not have the right to vote and could not make their voice heard in Parliament. In 1884, Parliament gave all men the right to vote and, for the first time, working men were able to have a say in the way Britain was run. A group of men who wanted to elect men from working class backgrounds to the House of Commons formed an 'Independent Labour Party'. In 1892, Kier Hardie, who had worked in a Scottish mine as a pit-boy, was elected MP for West Ham. In the twentieth century, the Labour Party grew to rival the long established Conservative and Liberal Parties.

It was with Queen Victoria's agreement that women were still denied the right to vote. She described the struggle for women's rights as 'this mad wicked folly'.

▲ When 700 women working at Bryant and May's match factory went on strike in 1888, they won a great deal of public sympathy.

Victorian Inventions

Before the 1870s, when the use of paraffin became widespread, Victorian houses were lit only by candles and oil lamps. Gas had been used for street lighting since 1814, but it took some years before it could be safely used in people's homes.

◀In the 1880s, gas began to be used to heat people's homes.

▶An advertisement for a washing machine.

▲Gas burners were placed on wall brackets and the light was improved by hoods called mantles which allowed the flame to give off a bright glow.

The use of electricity and the invention of the electric light bulb brought further improvements. In 1881, a few houses and streets were lit by electricity for the first time. Horse-drawn trams were soon replaced by faster and cleaner electric trams. Electricity also began to be used to send messages by telephone. The telephone was slow to catch on at first, because very few people could afford them, and many people were shy of using the new equipment.

Some Victorian inventions made housework easier. Carpet sweepers, which had to be pushed, used revolving brushes to pick up dirt. The first washing machines had blades which swung backwards and forwards to stir the water. The Singer Company made sewing machines which could be operated by a handle or treadle.

CWS·PELAW BOOT POLISH

The first typewriter to become generally available was made by the Remington Company in the United States. The first machines could only write in capital letters. By the end of the nineteenth century, they were being widely used in offices and businesses and provided work for thousands of women. Shorthand, a way of writing as quickly as a person can dictate, which was also widely used in office work, was invented by Isaac Pitman in 1837.

THE ROYAL BAR-LOCK

WRITES EVERY LETTER IN PLAIN SIGHT

HER MAJESTY'S TYPEWRITER MAKERS

Phosphorous-tipped matches known as 'Lucifers' were invented, which burst into flame when they were struck against sandpaper. Many people began to smoke paper-wrapped cigarettes instead of cigars and pipes. Men started to use the new 'safety razors' instead of the old-fashioned 'cut throat' razors. Women were able to buy artificially made perfumes for the first time.

Canned foods, which had been shown at the Great Exhibition in 1851 became available in the shops. The first cargo of refrigerated meat arrived from Australia in 1880. Refrigeration meant cheaper food and a more varied diet.

▼In 1877, Thomas Edison invented the phonograph or gramophone and recorded his own voice reciting 'Mary had a little lamb'.

The first car was invented in Queen Victoria's reign. By 1895, F. W. Lanchester had already set up a car factory in Birmingham. Within 30 years, the car had begun to affect the lives of everyone.

◄A family gathers around the piano to sing hymns. Victorian artists often drew idealistic rather than realistic pictures of family life.

A group of Christians known as the Evangelicals believed that the Church should be more concerned about the suffering of the poor. Their members included William Wilberforce, who had earlier fought to end slavery, and the factory reformer Lord Shaftesbury.

Members of a religious group called the Society of Friends were usually called Quakers because they called upon people to 'tremble at the word of the Lord'. Quaker families were among the best employers in Victorian Britain. They included Lloyd the banker and the chocolate manufacturers Fry, Cadbury and Rowntree. Some Quaker families went into the chocolate business because they wanted to improve the diet of the poor by providing bars of nourishment.

Churches and Chapels

Religion was an important part of Victorian life, although a religious census or survey carried out in 1851 revealed that only a third of the population attended church or chapel. Families who were religious considered Sunday to be 'the Lord's Day'. Everyone was expected to be very serious and solemn. Some children were not even allowed to read (except the Bible) or play with their toys.

The whole family went to church and sat in their own pew. Many families also held weekday prayers and said grace at every meal. The upper class mostly belonged to the Church of England but many middle and working class people went to Baptist and Methodist chapels, which were often thought of as centres of change and protest.

Some clergymen were the younger sons of gentry. Many of them seemed less interested in religion, than in the steady, comfortable job which was provided by the church. They competed with each other to become bishops and archbishops. In the countryside, the parson depended on the wealthy families of the parish for his income or 'living'. Town clergymen worked hard in their slum parishes to bring the Christian message to the poor. In the chapels, the ministers raged at their congregations and warned them of the 'fires of hell' which awaited them if they were not sober and God-fearing.

▲Church-going was often seen as an important social event. In this painting the congregation are leaving church after a Christening.

Christian Socialists thought that the government should do more to improve living and working conditions. Two of their famous members were the writers Charles Kingsley and Thomas Hughes. Kingsley's book 'The Water Babies' drew people's attention to the scandal of children being used to clean chimneys. Thomas Hughes' 'Tom Brown's Schooldays' described the brutality of some Victorian public schools.

In 1878, William Booth founded the Salvation Army. Booth had worked as a pawnbroker's assistant and seen the suffering of the poor. Salvation Army members wore uniforms, were known by military ranks and held open air meetings with bands and banners. The movement provided direct help for the needy. It ran night shelters, hostels and soup kitchens.

A great upset was caused in 1859 when the biologist Charles Darwin published his book the 'Origin of Species'. He cast doubt on the Victorians' unquestioning belief in the seven-day creation of the world as it is described in the Old Testament. Darwin argued instead that the development of man was the process of gradual change or evolution. He suggested that man had evolved from 'a hairy quadruped (four-legged animal), furnished with a tail and pointed ears, probably arboreal in its habits' – an ape. Darwin's view clashed with biblical teaching and the 'apes or angels' argument led to a storm of protest.

▲ In this Punch cartoon, which makes fun of the Victorian attitude to Darwin's theory, a gorilla arrives for dinner.

▼ A Salvation Army hostel in London, which provided shelter for homeless people.

At School

The Victorian ruling classes were not keen to educate working people. They thought that learning might encourage people to think about improving their lives by challenging the decisions of people in authority. Instead, they preferred to keep the workers in ignorance and 'not teach them to despise their lot in life'.

There was a hotchpotch of many different types of schools. There were the dame schools, run by old women from the parlours of their houses, charity schools, a few workhouse and factory schools and Sunday schools. Without books or proper teaching equipment, they taught only the basics of the 'Three Rs', reading, (w)riting and (a)rithmetic. The children of working class parents often had no chance to go to school because, at 6 and 7 years old, they were sent to work in the factories.

Middle class parents paid for their sons to go to grammar schools. These schools had been founded by kings, noblemen and merchants and were called grammar schools because their main aim was to teach Greek and Latin grammar. The sons of wealthy parents were sent to public schools like Rugby, Harrow and Winchester. In the early 1800s, public schools were known more for bullying and the riotous behaviour of their pupils than as places of learning. There were also private boarding schools like the dreadful Dotheboys Hall which Dickens wrote about in 'Nicholas Nickleby'.

▲ Many schools had only one classroom, so all the children were taught together. The room was sparsely furnished.

The daughters of middle class and wealthy parents were not sent to school, as it was not considered necessary for girls to be educated. Instead, these girls stayed at home and a governess taught them how to sew, sing and play the piano. These 'accomplishments' were thought to make a girl more likely to attract a husband.

British Schools and National Schools were started by churches and religious organisations throughout the country. They used the 'monitorial system', by which a teacher instructed the older pupils and they in turn taught the younger children. Learning was 'by rote', which meant that the class had to repeat their tables and answers in chorus.

▼ Dame schools often provided little more than a Victorian childminding service.

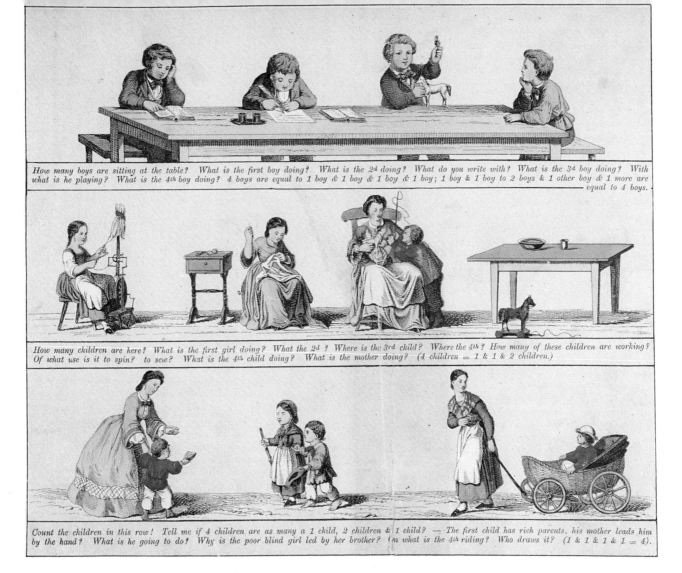

How many boys are sitting at the table? What is the first boy doing? What is the 2d doing? What do you write with? What is the 3d boy doing? With what is he playing? What is the 4th boy doing? 4 boys are equal to 1 boy & 1 boy & 1 boy & 1 boy; 1 boy & 1 boy to 2 boys & 1 other boy & 1 more are equal to 4 boys.

How many children are here? What is the first girl doing? What the 2d? Where is the 3rd child? Where the 4th? How many of these children are working? Of what use is it to spin? to sew? What is the 4th child doing? What is the mother doing? (4 children = 1 & 1 & 2 children.)

Count the children in this row! Tell me if 4 children are as many a 1 child, 2 children & 1 child? — The first child has rich parents, his mother leads him by the hand? What is he going to do? Why is the poor blind girl led by her brother? On what is the 4th riding? Who draws it? (1 & 1 & 1 & 1 = 4).

▲ A school book used in a Victorian classroom.

▼ A sewing class in a Board School. The simple desks have a shelf underneath to hold the pupils' books.

In 1858, teachers began to be 'paid by results'. This meant that a teacher's pay depended on how well his class did when they were questioned by an inspector. Teachers made children memorise lots of facts and, on the day of the inspector's visit, the slowest learners were encouraged to stay at home!

In 1870, Parliament passed an Education Act which said that all children should go to school from the age of five until they were ten years old. Boards were set up to provide schools in areas where there were none. Parents had to pay a few pence each week for their children to attend a Board School. This meant that the children of poorer parents were kept away from school.

Even in 1891, when Board Schools became free, some parents still did not allow their children to attend because they could not afford to lose the wages the children were earning in the factories. The factory workers also wanted their low-paid child labourers to continue working for them.

So the School Boards agreed to a 'half-time system'. Exhausted children were made to work in the factories until it was time for school. After school, they went back to the factory and worked until 10 pm. It was not until 1918 that Parliament stopped the 'half-time system' and forbade the employment of children under 12.

BLACKPOOL

Health & Pleasure, Glorious Sea

Through Bookings from the Principal Stations on the
MIDLAND · RAILWAY.

◀ As rail fares became cheaper, people began to travel further and more often. Families went on holidays and day trips to the seaside at Blackpool, Scarborough and Brighton.

▼ This drawing appeared in a newspaper report of a football match. Victorian footballs were made of leather and became very heavy in wet weather.

Leisure and Entertainment

Working people did not have much leisure time. After a ten hour working day, they were exhausted and content to spend the evening at home or in a local pub. Their only holidays were Sundays, Christmas Day and Good Friday. Even when they were not at work, they had no spare money to enjoy themselves.

During the second half of the century, employers began to allow their workers to have an extra half day off every week, usually Saturday afternoon. A few even allowed their workers to take an annual holiday, but they were not paid while they were away.

In 1871, a law allowed banks to close on Easter Monday, Whit Monday, the first Monday in August and Boxing Day. Once it was realised that little business could take place when the banks were closed, the days became public holidays – bank holidays.

◀ Large crowds visited the Epsom race-course on Derby Day. People from all classes of society gathered to watch the racing and enjoy a variety of track-side entertainments.

▲Tennis was a popular sport amongst the upper classes. Male players wore long trousers and women wore long-sleeved blouses and full-length skirts.

On their Saturday afternoons off, people enjoyed going to sporting events. Race meetings were popular and crowds of people travelled by train across the country to watch football matches. The first famous football clubs were church, chapel, school and factory sides. Queens Park Rangers began as Droop Street School and Manchester United was originally made up from men who worked for the Lancashire and Yorkshire Railway Company. The first FA Cup Final was played in 1872 between Wanderers and the Royal Engineers.

Although cricket started in the eighteenth century, the county championship only began in 1873. The most famous Victorian cricketer was W G Grace. During one cricket match, he refused to leave the field after being given out because he said the crowd had only come to see him bat!

Of course there was no television or radio in Victorian times, so people had to make their own entertainment. They had musical evenings and played parlour games. People enjoyed reading and, although there were no public libraries, it was possible to pay to borrow books. Novels were particularly popular, especially those of the great Victorian writers Charles Dickens, Charlotte and Emily Brontë, George Eliot and Thomas Hardy. Novels were often serialised in magazines in monthly parts.

At the theatre, people went to see the plays of Oscar Wilde and great actors and actresses such as Henry Irving and Mrs Patrick Campbell. The Savoy Theatre staged the comic operas of Gilbert and Sullivan.

The music hall was the most popular form of public entertainment. Every town had its music hall and in London there were 28! The cheapest seats which cost only a few pence were on a bench in the gallery, right at the top of the theatre. There were singers, comedians, acrobats and conjurors. One of the greatest music hall entertainers was Marie Lloyd, whose famous song was 'My old man said follow the van, don't dilly dally on the way'. By 1880, she was earning £100 a week, a fortune at that time.

▲A theatre programme from the 1890s. The cast list is bordered by advertisements for a variety of goods and services.

Trade and Empire

The British Empire included Canada, Australia, New Zealand, India, settlements in Africa and the Far East as well as many islands in the Caribbean and across the Pacific and Indian Oceans. Britain employed a huge army and navy to defend the empire and protect the trading arrangements between Britain and its overseas possessions. The colonies of the empire supplied Britain with goods like tea and cotton which Britain traded with other countries for a huge profit.

During Queen Victoria's reign, hundreds of thousands of British people emigrated to Canada, Australia and New Zealand. They were attracted by the prospect of plenty of open space to build their homes on, and the promise of a more relaxed and prosperous way of life, away from Britain's built up, crowded cities. In Canada, many British emigrants set up farms to grow wheat and raise cattle. Large amounts of grain, meat and timber were exported to Britain.

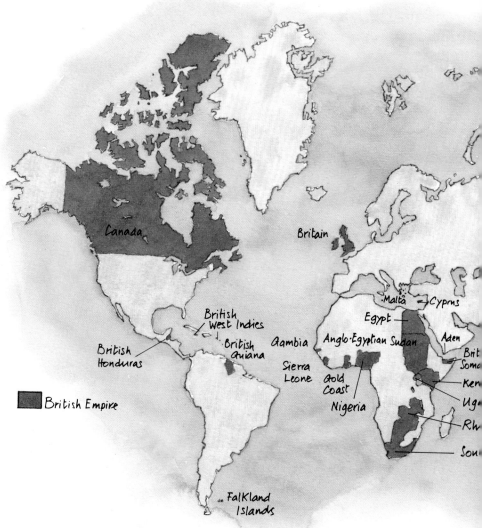

Canada — Britain — Malta — Cyprus — Egypt — Anglo-Egyptian Sudan — Aden — British West Indies — Gambia — British Honduras — British Guiana — Sierra Leone — Gold Coast — Nigeria — Falkland Islands — British Empire

▼ The 'Cutty Sark', a clipper ship built in 1869 which transported tea from China and later, wool from Australia to Britain. Today the ship can be seen in dry dock at Greenwich in South-East London.

▼ In this painting, called 'The Last of England', an emigrating couple take a last look at England before sailing abroad.

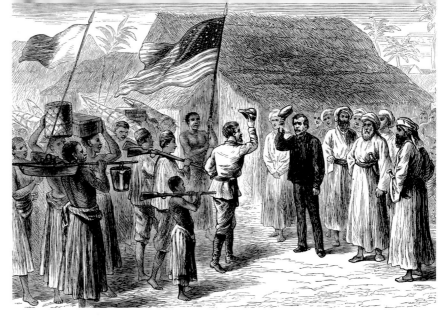

India was the 'jewel in the crown' of the British Empire. It was rich in natural resources like silk, cotton and tea. From the 1600s until 1858, India had been ruled by a private company, the East India Company. However, in 1857, thousands of Indians rebelled against British rule and tried to make their own choice of ruler Emperor of India. The British Army was used to bring the Indian Mutiny under control and from then on, the British government appointed representatives called viceroys to rule India. However, many Indians remained dissatisfied with British rule. In 1947, India became independent from Britain.

▲In the 1840s, David Livingstone began his exploration of Africa. In 1871, he was found by the explorer H M Stanley, after he had been missing for five years while searching for the source of the River Nile.

During the 1870s and 1880s, France, Germany and Britain competed to acquire territory in Africa as a way of expanding their empires. Britain gained the Gold Coast (now Ghana), Nigeria, Kenya and Uganda, and ruled over Egypt and the Sudan. From its African colonies, Britain was supplied with cocoa, coffee, teak and mahogany as well as diamonds from South Africa.

▼Britain was very proud of its empire. In this cartoon, the British lion is reviewing his troops – soldiers from Canada and Australia.

Until the 1840s, British criminals were transported to Australia. Convicts had to serve their sentences in areas where life was very hard where the land was not good enough to grow crops and food had to be rationed. After the 1840s, convicts were replaced by emigrants from Britain who greatly disrupted the lives of the native Aboriginals. Huge numbers of Aboriginals died from diseases which were spread by the settlers from Britain. Many British people did not succeed in Australia and died in poverty. Others became farmers and huge areas of land across Australia became used to rear sheep. Australia became wealthy by exporting wool and mutton as well as gold, which was discovered there in 1851.

In 1840 in New Zealand, Maori chiefs signed the Treaty of Waitangi with settlers from Britain. This made New Zealand part of the British Empire.

A Woman's Place?

Working class Victorian women worked alongside the men on the farms and in the factories and mills. Many women were employed as 'sweated labour' in cramped workshops in attics and cellars which badly affected their health. The regulations of the Factory Acts did not apply to these squalid 'sweat shops' where women worked all day stitching garments for a few pence. One Victorian song protests about the sufferings of these women:

> 'Stitch! Stitch! Stitch!
> In poverty, hunger and dirt.
> Sewing at once with a double thread
> A shroud as well as a shirt'.

By the end of the century, domestic service had become the main occupation of working class women. Middle class women had a wider choice since they could become nurses, governesses or schoolteachers. They were untrained and were paid very badly. Upper class women did not work. With nannies to look after their children and servants to run their homes, they were expected to be devoted and obedient wives.

> 'Man for the field and woman for the hearth;
> Man for the sword, and for the needle she;
> Man with the head, and woman with the heart;
> Man to command, and woman to obey'.
>
> *Tennyson: The Princess*

▲ A painting called 'The Labourer's Welcome' illustrating the Victorian opinion that 'a woman's place is in the home'. A wife sews as she waits obediently for her husband to return from work.

▼ Many street vendors were women who sold flowers from barrows. In this painting, a flower seller offers a posy to a child from a wealthy family who is out walking with her mother or nanny.

The education of girls was considered to be a waste of time and this made it impossible for them to follow a career.

In Victorian times, women were thought to be inferior to men. Women were refused the right to vote. A married woman was not allowed to own property. Everything that she owned or inherited belonged to her husband. If a man left his wife, he did not have to provide her with any money to live on. It was impossible by law for a woman to divorce her husband.

During the 1880s, the situation began to improve. Laws were passed which stated that women could own property and had to be provided for if their husbands left them. Women began to train as nurses, following the example set by Florence Nightingale during the Crimean War. When education became compulsory, the demand for teachers increased and more women began to enter the profession. The invention of the telephone and typewriter created more job opportunities for women in office work.

Long skirts were not suitable for cycling to work, so some women began to wear bloomers; long baggy knickers named after their American designer, Amelia Bloomer. Bloomers gave women greater independence by replacing the long skirts which had restricted their movements.

▲ A huge demonstration against the admission of women to a Cambridge college. The banner warns that it is 'no place for you maids'.

In 1848, the first college for women was opened in London. It was called Queen's College. Two students of the college, Frances Buss and Dorothea Beale, went on to found schools for girls. In 1870, Elizabeth Garrett Anderson finally overcame years of male prejudice to qualify as the first woman doctor. One of the great Victorian campaigners for women's voting rights was Lydia Becker. She worked tirelessly to set up suffrage societies but failed to win the right for women to vote. It was not until 1928 that all women over the age of 21 finally won the right to vote.

► The opportunities for office work greatly increased during the late 1800s. Many women found jobs as clerks and typists.

Time Chart:

	1830s	1840s	1850s	1860s
Inventions and Events	**1837:** Pitman invents shorthand **1839:** The first Grand National is run	**1840:** The Penny Post is started by Rowland Hill **1843:** The 'Great Britain', designed by Isambard Kingdom Brunel, becomes the first steamship to cross the Atlantic Ocean; the first public telegraph system is set up between Paddington and Slough.	**1851:** The Great Exhibition takes place in Crystal Palace; in the United States, Singer invents the first practical sewing machine.	**1861:** Horse-drawn trams are used for the first time **1863:** The first underground railway opens in London
People	**1837:** Accession of Queen Victoria	**1840:** Marriage of Queen Victoria and Prince Albert **1842:** Social reformer Edwin Chadwick writes a report condemning inadequate sanitation in industrial towns **1844:** The 'Rochdale Pioneers' set up the first co-operative shop **1847:** James Simpson discovers that chloroform can be used as an anaesthetic **1849:** David Livingstone begins his exploration of central Africa	**1851:** A religious census reveals that only one third of Britain's population attends a church or chapel **1854:** Publication of 'Hard Times' by Charles Dickens describing the appalling living and working conditions for poor people in industrial towns **1855:** Florence Nightingale saves hundreds of lives by improving the conditions of hospital wards at Scutari during the Crimean War **1857:** Publication of 'Tom Brown's Schooldays' by Thomas Hughes **1859:** Publication of 'The Origin of Species' by Charles Darwin	**1861:** Prince Albert dies of typhoid fever **1863:** Publication of 'The Water Babies' by Charles Kingsley **1867:** Dr Barnado founds his 'East End Mission' for homeless children; Joseph Lister uses his carbolic antiseptic in surgery
Reforms and Politics	**1838:** The People's Charter is drawn up	**1842:** The Mines Act prohibits the employment of women and young children underground **1847:** The Ten Hours Act limits working hours for women and children to ten hours a day; the scandal of the Andover workhouse is exposed **1848:** Women are admitted to London University; Chartists' petition found to include many faked signatures	**1854:** The Crimean War begins **1856:** The County and Borough Police Act makes it compulsory for every county in Britain to have a paid police force **1857:** The Indian Mutiny **1859:** Parliament allows peaceful picketing during strikes	**1862:** The 'payment by results' system is introduced in schools **1864:** The Climbing Boys Act makes it illegal to use young boys as chimney sweeps **1868:** The first Trade Union Congress takes place in Manchester

1870s	1880s	1890s	1900s
1871: Bank Holidays are introduced in Britain **1872:** The first FA Cup final is played **1873:** The cricket county championships begin **1874:** In the United States, Remington manufactures the first typewriter **1876:** Bell invents the telephone **1877:** Edison invents the gramophone **1878:** The 'Red Flag' Act fixes the maximum speed for vehicles at 4 mph	**1880:** The first cargo of refrigerated meat arrives from Australia **1881:** Houses and streets are lit by electricity for the first time	**1891:** Electric trams begin running in London **1895:** X-rays are first demonstrated by Wilhelm Röntgen **1896:** Marconi demonstrates his wireless in Britain	**1900:** Britain builds 75% of all the world's steamships; Britain's railway network covers 29,000 kilometres of track
1870: Elizabeth Garrett Anderson qualifies as a doctor **1871:** Gilbert and Sullivan begin writing comic operas **1878:** William Booth founds the Salvation Army	**1885:** Marie Lloyd makes her first stage appearance **1888:** Port Sunlight is built for the workers in the Lever brothers' factory	**1892:** Kier Hardie becomes the first member of the Independent Labour Party to be elected to Parliament **1896:** Alfred Harmsworth founds the Daily Mail **1897:** Queen Victoria's Diamond Jubilee	**1901:** Queen Victoria dies
1870: The Education Act states that School Boards are to be set up to provide elementary schools where they do not already exist **1872:** The Ballot Act allows voting to take place in secret; The Public Health Act makes the appointment of medical officers of health compulsory **1874:** The Factory Act raises the minimum working age to nine **1875:** The Artisans' Dwelling Act allows councils to take over and clear slum housing; the Matrimonal Causes Act allows wives to divorce their husbands **1876:** Medical schools are opened to women	**1880:** School attendance is made compulsory up to the age of ten **1882:** The Married Woman's Property Act gives women the rights to property belonging to them before marriage and to their earnings from work **1884:** The Reform Act gives adult males the right to vote **1886:** Gladstone fails to pass the Irish Home Rule Bill **1888:** Match girls from the Bryant and May factory go on strike in London **1889:** London dockers go on strike for a basic wage of sixpence an hour; the Boer War begins	**1890:** Parliament allows councils to use money from the rates to build council houses **1891:** The Factory Act raises the minimum working age to 11; Elementary education is made free **1893:** Gladstone's Home Rule Bill is rejected again **1897:** The first suffragette groups are formed **1899:** The school leaving age is raised to 12 	

The End of an Era

'The world is gone for me', wrote Queen Victoria when Albert died in 1861, yet she was to reign for a further 40 eventful years. She withdrew from public life and spent most of her time at Balmoral in Scotland. She refused to attend state occasions, which caused many people to question whether it was worthwhile having a monarchy at all.

Towards the end of Victoria's reign, working and living conditions for working class people were improving, but many people still lived in poverty. Scientific advances affected people's lives differently.

From the 1870s, steam ships had been bringing cargoes of cheap grain to Britain from North America. Ten years later, ships carrying frozen meat from Australia and Argentina began arriving. Prices of food dropped and town workers could afford a better diet. However, many British farmers went out of business because they could not afford to compete with this cheap food from abroad. As a result, many farm workers lost their jobs.

◄Queen Victoria towards the end of her reign.

▼There was still a great deal of poverty in Britain at the end of the Victorian era. These barefoot children were photographed in London in the 1890s.

Between 1845 and 1849 the potato crop in Ireland was ruined by a blight. This caused a famine, during which thousands of people died. The Irish blamed the British government for their suffering. The potato famine greatly increased the number of Irish people who wanted to gain independence from Britain. Some joined the Fenian Brotherhood and were prepared to use force to win 'Home Rule'. When Gladstone first became prime minister he said, 'My mission is to pacify Ireland'. In 1886 and again in 1893, he tried to pass a law which would give Ireland Home Rule but he failed and the 'Irish problem' remained unresolved.

As the years passed, Queen Victoria's popularity returned and in 1897 she celebrated the sixtieth year of her accession. The Diamond Jubilee was marked by scenes of wild enthusiasm.

During Victoria's reign which spanned 64 years, Britain passed through a period of great industrial growth, expanded a vast empire overseas and became the wealthiest and most powerful nation in the world. After Victoria's death in 1901, Britain faced the future with uncertainty. Few people could remember a time when Victoria had not been queen.

▲ An Irish Catholic peasant family are turned out of their home by a representative of their Protestant landlord. Houses were often burned to the ground to prevent them being re-occupied.

The situation in Ireland remained an insoluble problem throughout Victoria's reign. One eighth of the population were Protestants, but they owned all the land. The majority of Irish people were Roman Catholic and peasants. The land on which they lived and worked was owned by 'absentee landlords'. These men often lived in England and employed agents to collect the rent from their tenants. These tenant farmers lived in extreme poverty and were constantly afraid of falling into debt and being evicted from their homes.

▼ Traffic chaos at Piccadilly Circus at the turn of the century. Among the horse-drawn vehicles can be seen an increasing number of more modern motorbuses and taxis.

Index

This index will help you to find some of the important things in *How We Used to Live*. The page numbers shown in **dark letters** refer to illustrations.